Journey Through Jesus

Bringing Heaven to Earth

Stacy B. Natzel

Contents

Dedication

I dedicate this book to my Heavenly Father, and to my family and friends. If it were not for their encouragement, love, and support, I would not have been confident in sharing my experience.

I hope my book will offer inspiration for those seeking faith, or those who are already a follower of Christ.

I believe we are all messengers from God if we choose to be, and we all have something valuable to share with each other.

Endorsement

"Stacy's writings reverberate with her passionate desire to know God and to integrate him into every aspect of her life. Stacy's heartfelt pondering and insights will encourage you to fall more deeply in love with God."

Michael White, Senior Pastor at Harbor Covenant Church

Prologue

What does it mean to live a Godly life in today's society? There are many different religions and Christian denominations, and each one teaches their version of who God is. There is only one God, so when did God become divided? God has never changed and never will, so why are we trying to change God? The question is, who is GOD?

I have met many people throughout my life that have claimed to be a Christian, but they didn't portray Godly characteristics. Does someone know God because they go to church every Sunday, or partake in religious traditions?

I thought of myself as a Christian for most of my life, until I realized it was just a facade. I filled my life with meaningless things void of real fulfillment.

Chasing after the world becomes tiresome and leads to nothing but an empty heart. Instant gratifications are what they are–they only last but an instant, and then we are back to wanting more. What are we searching for? What is our main focus in life? Do our lives revolve around us or God? Seeking God comes from within and not from outside influences. Only after making a commitment to God, will we then have a true desire to live for God, and we will not think of it as work, but rather a way of life that makes us who we were created to be. Within all of us is our true selves, and we discover who we are the moment we trust God.

When we cry out to God, He comforts us, and by accepting Jesus, it means we accept God's gift to us when He sacrificed His Son to save us all from the sins we carry.

Jesus has revealed Himself to many people throughout the world, and the Bible is not the only testimony there is.

After my experience, I knew what happened to me was real, so I went on a search to find others that had similar experiences. I was astonished to find that they had learned the same things I did.

My experience lead me to the truth. The truth that we are all connected. When I saw visions of heaven, I saw that we are all LOVE, and there are no burdens that separate us. We are all connected to each other and God is our Father. We are connected telepathically to His glorious light, which is our SUN in heaven. Jesus is our lord and savior, and we walk with Him along beautiful grassy meadows.

As a true disciple of Jesus, all we are supposed to do is show people love, because God is love.

Practicing love takes time and patience and we will never be perfect, but God doesn't expect us to be. Our journey on this earth is full of hardships, but God gives us the strength to get through them. It is not our mission to change others, but instead to change ourselves, by growing in love, and to always remember that we have a never changing perfect loving God.

My Walk With Jesus

I will never forget the day I was saved by God's grace. I knew at one time in my life I felt His presence when I was younger, but over time, as I went through my late adolescence and into my 20s, God was very distant. Not because He abandoned me, but because I was too busy for God and I turned my back on him. I was living my life the way I wanted to.

I stopped praying, because I did not feel worthy, and I lived my life this way for about eighteen years. At times, I would break down because I felt so lost. During that time, I tried my best to be a good mother and advance in my cooking career, but I endured a lot of failure. I put pressure on myself to do whatever I could to take care of my family, and I tried doing it all without God's help.

I did not like how I was living, and I felt there was always an empty void in my life that I was not able to fill. Although my husband and son were my whole world, I felt that we were just going through the motions, and I was unable to grasp my real purpose in life.

One day I got a call from my sister, Jacquelyn, and she was going through a very hard time. Her husband was diagnosed with leukemia, and she told me she needed my help. I went to visit her in Washington State, where I am from. During my visit, I took care of my niece and helped cook meals, while my sister took care of her husband in the hospital. When she got home every evening, we spent time together talking, and she pulled out her Bible and read passages to me. I saw how much her faith was helping her through the difficult time in her life. I remember thinking how strong she was, and I admired her perseverance. She told me that her strength came from God. I was instantly brought back to reality, as I started to realize what I was missing in my life. While I was busy helping my sister, my son was staying at his grandmother's house. I went to pick him up, so I could spend a couple days with him. I took him to my mother's house, and I didn't seem to notice a spider bite that he was itching on his leg.

His leg became very infected, and I had to rush him to the hospital. The doctor told me that it was a serious staph infection and that he was lucky that I brought him in when I did. As I sat there with my son in the hospital for two days, I found myself with nothing to do but think. I remember the bondage I felt at that moment, about the choices I had been making, and I felt so selfish for taking so much for granted in my life. As my son lay there hooked up to IVs, I cried and felt helpless. I thought about my sister and how she was sitting next to her husband in another hospital just miles away.

I dropped to my knees and started sobbing. I cried out to God. *Wasn't there a time when you were there, God?* Yes, there was. I remembered a time when I was 14 years old. My cousin and best friend, Phaedra, had just passed away. I remembered it was the most difficult time in my life as a child, but I remembered how I got through it.

We moved to a new town and I struggled making new friends. My parents were also distant to me, because I had younger siblings that needed their full attention. My step-dad decided to enroll me into ski school for the winter.

After ski class they would let us go off and ski by ourselves, and I remember even though I spent a lot of time alone, I did not feel alone. I remember sitting on top of the snow-covered mountain and I could feel God's presence. I remember I felt a sense of peacefulness, and I would talk to him. *Yes, I remember, God, you were always there! What happened?*

I cried out, "I am so sorry for turning my back on you, please forgive me! I want to have you in my life again, and feel your love, like I did on top of that mountain." I prayed on my knees sobbing on the hospital floor. I felt God's love surround me in my utter humiliation. I cried out to Jesus to save me and save my son. I pictured Jesus in my mind, and I imagined myself dropping down to His feet, praying for Him to take control of my heart. I instantly felt comforted and I could feel God's loving embrace. I knew at that moment I was different, because I did not feel the empty void I once felt, and I was seeing everything with new eyes. I knew that I needed to make changes in my life, but I knew it would take time. The fear I once had was replaced by a sense of comfort, as if Jesus was there holding my hand.

I went back to Huntington Beach, California, where we lived, and told my husband that we needed to move to Las Vegas, where his mom lived, so I could go back to school. I asked God to help guide my future, and I came up with a business idea and had tremendous determination to achieve it.

The three years we spent in Las Vegas were very difficult, but I never lost faith and I never gave up. I finished school and eventually opened my business, but I could feel God drifting from my life. My husband and I were drifting apart, and I was putting my business before anything else in my life. I would cry myself to sleep almost every night, because I wanted my business to do well, so we could save up enough money to have a baby.

We decided to move back to Washington State. I prayed, and I could feel that it was the right thing to do, and I had a feeling my business would do better in my hometown of Gig Harbor.

Once we moved back, my husband and I were finally blessed with our baby girl. I had been praying for our little girl for seven years, and I always knew I would have her because I never lost faith. I realized that it was all on God's timing and seeing such a miracle made my faith grow even stronger.

I took some time off to spend with our new child, and my son was doing well by getting involved in our local church. I reopened my business and was finding myself with less time to spend with God. I would try to pray every night, but my prayers seemed very complacent and redundant. I spent countless nights in dismay and heartbroken over the evil in the world. I kept asking God why. I asked him how someone could do something so awful. *Is all sin the same, God, or isn't some sin unforgivable?*

When I thought about certain people, I compared what they had done to my own wrongdoing. I cried about my past, when I too was lost at one time and did not have God in my life to help guide me. Is it their fault? How could they possibly know if they are blind? Without God, how can anyone see their wrongdoing? I cried out, not only for the victims in our world, but also for the blind and lost souls. *Can you please help them see, God?*

I kept waking up every morning, and I did not feel like I was doing anything in my life to help make a difference, so I said a prayer I had never prayed before. In deep prayer and with my whole heart and soul, I dropped down to my knees and cried out to God, "I want to be a true disciple of Jesus Christ. I want to help the world. Will you please use me?" I cried, "I surrender my life to your will, to do your works."

In my heart, I felt God urge me to read my Bible. During the next month, all I did was read my Bible in between taking care of my responsibilities and work. I highlighted passages, and I read not in one place, but all over the Bible. I started to notice God guiding me. I had read the Bible in the past, but this was the first time I was fully dedicated in understanding God's way of life. God helped me understand everything I was reading, and

I felt myself finally able to understand who God was.

During the last week of reading my Bible in full dedication, I was not that interested in eating. I ate enough to be satisfied, but I did not let myself get too full. I also started thanking God for each meal that I ate, which is something I never did before. When I wasn't reading my Bible, I was constantly praying to God, and I reached a state of euphoria. I was able to see the strongholds in my life. Any past regret or grudge I had kept in was holding my heart captive. Every time I found a stronghold, I cried out for God to forgive me.

When I was able to free myself from the strongholds, I realized the compassion I was able to have for others and how much I could freely love everyone around me. I got to a point where I was afraid to make a mistake, and I was so worried that if I did, I would disappoint God. I felt myself hitting a wall, because I knew it was impossible to be perfect.

I woke up the next morning and I could hear God's voice. He was in control of my mind. He showed me how much He loved me. I laid there in my bed, with tears of joy streaming down my face. I met God's presence. I could not see Him, but I could feel His love. In disbelief, in my mind I talked to God. He took me on a journey through my mind. He took me to a place in my upper subconscious, where I could speak to Him directly through thought. The thoughts were so powerful that I could actually hear God's voice. He talked to me as a father would. I could not believe what was happening. All I could think was, *Why me? I am not important.* God instantly helped me understand how important I was to Him. He poured His love into me, and I could feel He was my Father, but a Father with more love than I had ever known. I kept weeping and kept thinking over and over, *You love me that much? Me?* He poured more love into me, and there are no words to describe the amount of love I felt. He told me that I had been crying out for the world as He does, and that I have

His heart. I could feel His whole heart and how much love He has for everyone in the world.

I asked God questions. "Who are you, God?"

He answered, "I AM that I AM."

"Who is Jesus?"

He answered, "WE ARE that WE ARE."

I asked God, "Who am I?"

He answered, "You are my child."

"Who is everyone else?"

He answered, "You are all of my children. We are that we are."

"What are we, God?"

He answered, "WE ARE LOVE."

More tears streamed down my face in utter humility and joy. I had so many questions, and I felt frantic to ask as many as I could, but could not find the words. God told me that I must seek His face before every thought or action. He told me before starting my day to talk to Him and He would tell me what to do. When God told me to rest, I was supposed to rest. He would control my mind, and He took me through layers of my consciousness. He took me to the lowest layer where I could still feel his presence, but I was sound asleep, and I could feel my body completely relaxed. It was like God was in control of my whole being, and I was a long for the ride.

God showed me pictures in the lowest layer, and He showed me things I was to choose from. I felt myself being judged, but not in a bad way. I would see things in the world that were good and things in the world that were bad, and I rejected the bad images and chose the good ones. I didn't understand why, but God was putting me through some sort of test. He was trying to show me who I was and what my heart desired. I didn't feel like I was in my body at times.

I asked God about heaven, and he said, "It is truly a paradise, my child."

I asked God who was in heaven. He told me, "We are already there, for there is no time in heaven, so everyone that is supposed to be in heaven is there."

I asked God if I could see heaven. God showed me visions of heaven and it was a place I had always dreamed of. I saw some of my family members and that we lived in a large kingdom. My husband and I lived in a castle and my whole family shared it. My son and my sister, Naomi, were kinsman, God told me. I saw that they were best friends, and only love and strong leadership qualities flowed out from their eyes. I was so proud of my son in heaven, because he was everything I knew he could always be, and I cried with so much joy. I saw my sister, Jacquelyn, and she took care of many children. I could not see very much, because God told me that I could only see glimpses into heaven.

I asked God if I could talk to people I knew.

He said, "Yes, we are all connected through thought in heaven."

I asked God, "What do we do? Don't we get bored?"

He laughed, and I said, "You know how to laugh, Father?"

He said, "Yes, my child."

He told me that we all have the same gifts in heaven as we are given on Earth, and we have duties, but we do them joyfully. Everyone knows each other's hearts in heaven, and although we remember our lives on Earth, there is no judgement, resentment, fear, jealousy, hostility, or shame. Only love, joy, and laughter.

I could feel my burdens keeping me from experiencing the joy I was supposed to feel, and I felt sad because of it. God told me that I carried many burdens and that He must heal them. He showed me how to search my whole heart, until I would ask, "Father, why do I feel that way?" He would wait until I discovered each burden that I carried, but He would not do it for me. He was patient with me until I discovered what they were. It was not able to all be done in one day, so He would tell me it was time to start my day.

God told me He would tell me what to do each moment. I had to ask Him before I did anything.

I sometimes forget to ask God for my next step. I would do things on my own, and I would grow weary. I asked, "Father what happens when I forget to ask you for my next step? Are you mad?"

He answered, "No, my child, I am not mad. When you do your own will, you will only lose time, many shortcomings come from that."

I said, "Father, I am tired." He gave me strength when I asked for it.

I felt my chest get heavy. I asked, "Why do I feel that way?"

He answered, "They are burdens you are carrying. You must discover what they are and let go of them." He showed me that each time I discovered a burden, I could not let it go without asking for forgiveness. I would ask God to forgive me and then Jesus would redeem me.

I rested again that day as my daughter took a nap. I asked God, "What do I do now?"

He took me to a resting place where He could speak to me again more clearly. He told me this is a place where I could ask him questions, and we could connect. He showed me more burdens I carried, but He had to go deep into my subconscious to reach them.

He told me that it is not our fault for the burdens we carry, because they are passed down to us from many generations. He explained that since He loves all of His children, He wants to free us all from the sins we carry. He said we are all guilty, but no one is to blame. He said we must not blame anyone, but forgive and love one another to help heal others' burdens and our own. He told me that the children of His who feel the burdens and want to change need forgiveness from others to help them. He explained that I could not forgive someone with my words, but with my whole heart and God's heart.

The next day was the day of the eclipse, and I didn't want to see it. After the eclipse was over, I got up and got dressed to go to my mother's house to visit. On my drive over, I looked up at the sun shining, and I could see it for the first time in my life, without being blinded by it. I saw the sun and wept with joy. I could feel God's love shining through the sun, and He was allowing me to look right at Him. I was filled with so much love that my compassion for everyone around me was overflowing.

I went into my mom's house and I saw things I had never noticed before. I had a new sense of smell, and I could smell good and evil all around me. I went outside to the patio where my mother was sitting, and I tried to explain what I had been going through. I felt too excited to share the news, and it was not making sense to her. I could feel my experience was something no one would understand and that I would have a hard time expressing it to anyone.

I went home, and tried telling my husband what I had been going through, but he didn't understand. I had kept it in, because God had told me not to tell anyone, but instead to write it down, but I did not listen. Since my husband didn't believe what I was telling him, I started to get upset. I just wanted him to believe me, and the more upset I got, the more alone I felt.

My new senses overwhelmed me, and I could not only smell unusual things, but at night I could see evil. I woke up in the middle of the night, and I could see red eyes staring at me. Fear gripped my heart, and I yelled at the evil faces laughing at me in horrifying torment, but my fear only seemed to feed their energy, and make them stronger. I cried out to God, and He could not help me because, as He reminded me, I had to let go of my fear and trust Him, but I was too afraid. I lost many nights of sleep and got very sick.

I felt myself slipping into a deep hole, and fear consumed me. God's voice was very distant, and in my heart, He was urging me to be strong. I laid there paralyzed by fear, not able to move my body. I could feel God fighting for me, but I was trapped in darkness and could no longer feel God's love or hear Him.

God told me in a small voice that He was coming to get me, and I waited there for what seemed like an eternity. A light came, and I felt myself being lifted out of the darkness, but I saw evil faces all around me. God told me to focus on the light and His Love, and to chant to myself "I am love" over and over again. Finally, I reached the top and could feel God's presence. Jesus came to me, and I instantly felt comforted and safe.

I did not understand what had happened to me. The feeling of being in that awful place was more than I could bare to recall. I was no longer there, but the thought of that place scared me so much, I was in complete agony. It was a place without love, hope, joy, or comfort, and God was not there. I started to realize that I had been attacked by evil and since my body was weak, it had consumed me. God reminded me to focus on Him and that love is my weapon against the enemy, which is FEAR. He told me to rest and not be afraid, because the enemy will attack you with fear when your body is weak.

I let myself trust God, and a sense of peacefulness came over me, I saw stone steps and I was in some type of changing room. I was no longer in my body, but I felt more alive than before. I felt a sense of excitement, as if it were the day of my wedding and a joyous occasion awaited me. God told me that it was not my time yet and that I had a mission to help others. I asked God, "How can I help anyone, when I am only one person?" He let me know that during my lifetime, I would help a lot of people.

I said, "Father, what if I fail you?"

He said, "You will not fail, because everyone you helped is already here." His words were thoughts, and they permeated my presence, as if I was soaking in knowledge. The peacefulness I felt was indescribable, and I did not want to leave, because I knew I was finally home. I didn't understand why I had to leave when God told me everyone was already in this place. God's concept of time did not make sense for me to put into words. He must have been speaking of the future, but as I lingered in God's presence, time seemed to stand still. Time itself seemed interconnected in a way that God was able to see right through it. God told me to be strong, and I was instantly back in my body.

I opened my eyes, and paramedics were all around me. My husband had called the ambulance—when he had found me, I wasn't breathing. I was covered in sweat and urine and felt crippled by my humiliation.

I let out a cry as if my whole world came crashing down on me. My body was weak, and I kept weeping because I no longer felt the peacefulness I had felt when I was with God, and I could no longer hear his voice in my mind. I was rushed to the hospital. They ran a CAT scan on me, and all the results came back normal.

My husband got to the hospital and he told me he was sorry for not believing me. I told him it was real, and he understood. He told me he would take care of me so I could get better. We went home, and my husband had to feed me and bathe me because I was so weak. I remembered what God had told me. He told me that my husband would be my voice of reason and to let him guide me.

I remembered what I had learned when I was in God's presence, and it was running through my mind. I closed my eyes and played the visions over and over again, in hopes that I would not forget what I had learned.

I saw a vison of how God created the universe. The whole universe was created through his thought. I saw that one thought of a perfect soul was all it took for life to take place. He thought, and life exploded into existence. He had not meant for evil to get into our world, and since He knew the future, He needed to save us all from sin and suffering.

He told me that I was carrying burdens from the world by worrying about others, but it was not my burden to carry. God showed me that we are all connected, and the burdens that we carry separate us from each other and from Him. He explained that since we live in a world of sin, there is no escaping it. Sin is everywhere, so the only way to escape it is through eternal life. He said, "I gave you the gift of eternal life by overcoming the world through Jesus and taking on all of your burdens."

God showed me that when he created the universe, we were all stars, and He picked my star out of the night sky and held it in between His fingers. He showed me that He created each one of our souls and poured them into each star, and that those stars would one day ignite our souls in our mortal bodies on Earth. He showed me that my daughter Lily was my dream, my vision, and I created her through perfect love and perfect faith, because I never gave up on having her. He held her star in the palm of His hand, and He told me she was special, and I needed to protect her and be strong for her.

Then God showed me that her perfect soul would one day be tempted by evil, because evil was in the world. I cried, "No God please I don't want her to be evil." He showed me that in the beginning, He mourned for His children, and He did not want any of His children to be corrupted by the evil in the world because He loves us all equally. God then asked me who, between my two children,

I would sacrifice to save the other. I cried, "No, God, I can't choose, please don't make me. Take me instead!" I felt God's pain envelop me as I cried out for my children, and I could feel His love for them far exceeded my own. God showed me that is what He did for us. He sacrificed Himself in the flesh through His Son Jesus Christ, because Jesus would be willing, and He needed a willing soul to fulfill His will.

I finally understood God's plan for all of humanity and His timing for us all. "What happens then, Father? I don't want anyone to suffer eternal death." He told me His plan will demolish all evil, and by the end of time, there will be more good than evil, and good will prevail. He said, "Thy will be done, thy Kingdom come."

That evening I laid there with my husband, and I held his hand as we drifted off to sleep. I could feel my husband's breath enter my lungs. I could feel we were connected as one through our hearts. I knew at that moment what it would feel like with him, when we left this earth and went to our eternal home, and I was no longer afraid. I could no longer hear God's voice, and I felt lost. I did not know what my next step was. I felt as though I had to learn who I was again. Without God, who am I? I finally understood what God was revealing to me at that very moment. He had not left me, nor had He ever. He was still a part of my consciousness, and I had to start trusting myself, so I could begin my mission to grow in LOVE.

Reflection

Before my experience, I had faith in God, but after knowing God and becoming one with Him, I was able to see everything through His eyes for a brief period of time. I was free for once in my life. I was free from shame, fear, and was encompassed in pure intentional LOVE. I felt a love I had never known or felt in this life, and I was a part of it. I met an intelligent loving Father, and I could see others as He does.

After coming back, I was disappointed to say the least. My life was shattered, because I was in complete peace and I knew I was going home. I knew had to come back for my children, for my husband, for others that God told me that I was supposed to help. I was told I had a mission in this life, as we all do.

I was in a place free from time, free from any earthly desire, free from the burdens that we have to carry throughout our mortal lives. I was given knowledge beyond words, as all of creation and why we are here flashed before my eyes. Knowledge beyond any comprehension we are able to grasp with our earthly minds. A knowledge that transcends everything that I once thought was important, which no longer held value, because the meaning of life is so much more.

I was finally safe and I no longer had to worry about the trivial things in my past life. A beautiful three-dimensional new world, more vivid and real than any earthly place I had ever known. A family without divide and without rules of the mundane life. Seeing others as they were created to be and knowing that we are all connected through love and we are love.

Coming back to my body felt as though I had a cold, wet blanket thrown over me, and I was trapped in my mortal mind, constricted by a dimension in which I was forced to look at everything through a tiny, one-dimensional hole. No longer fearing death, but longing for the day I would be reunited with my true self, and others as we are all one love.

Being forced to follow a life governed by time. Forced back into a world of complete chaos. Having to wear a mask around everyone to fit in. Wanting more than anything to cure the suffering and the pain in the world, by reassuring everyone that everything will be okay, because one day we will all be going home. Wanting to help people understand that money, possessions, looks, religious rules, politics—none of that means anything.

Wanting everyone to be real and show their true emotions, and to stop walking around in fear of love, in fear of loving themselves, in fear of showing their scars. Accepting that we are not who we think we are, because we are so much more than what others have told us we are supposed to be.

I knew I must keep living each day and keep trying to get back to knowing who I once was, but also trying my hardest to love everyone, as I once was able to when I became the essence of love itself.

After my experience, I had a hard time trying to figure out what had happened to me. I was given a wealth of knowledge, but I felt crippled by the pressure for it to make sense.

My comprehension was limited by my human brain, and although I understood the messages and visions when I received them, my understanding was blocked by the nature of my human reasoning.

What I had a very hard time grasping was why God had allowed me to fall into such a deep pit of despair. It was like my whole consciousness entered into a dimension of unfathomable evil, where I became fear itself. I could still sense my body, but my mind was in a different realm where time did not exist and I was trapped in darkness. As I started piecing together my experience, I realized God rescued me out of the darkness only to show me that He did not put me there. I had put myself there, but how?

I gave into fear and allowed it to consume me, and I wasn't allowing myself to trust God's love. What I realized is that God does not separate himself from us. We separate ourselves from God by allowing evil to enter into our consciousness, not forgiving ourselves, feeling unworthy of God's love, giving into fear, or having bad intentions. Just by thinking in this manner, our thoughts are entering into a dark dimension where God does not reside.

I also came to realize that I had experienced love far more powerful than I could have ever imagined, and a love for others that is not possible to feel where good and evil coexist in our space time dimension. I had one foot in this world and another foot in a spiritual realm.

I experienced heaven on Earth as well as hell on Earth and was stuck in the middle of the spiritual warfare as it was playing tug-of-war with my soul. When I saw others around me, while walking between both worlds, I was able to see how easily people were manipulated by the evil lurking in every corner. When someone was angry, I could feel their energy going into the air and evil entities would be drawn to it, as if the enemy depended upon using others as his personal puppets.

I saw that the evil inside others was not so much a part of them, but was a part of the enemy, and I saw people for the way God intended them to be. I started to wonder, since these demonic entities were able to consume me because of my fear, then how many others had they taken over and manipulated in order to create more chaos in our world?

Before I was attacked by fear, I remembered God had showed me a series of images, and I wondered why I felt it was God judging me? It was like a slideshow, and attached to each image were my emotions.

Just by reacting to the images displayed before me in my mind, I knew I was attracted to good and not evil, and my thoughts displayed what my heart and soul yearned for. What I learned is that we are the ones who judge ourselves, and we choose between good and evil.

Evil and carnal things are earth-bound, but when we die, our spirits are set free from our mortal bodies and our freedom allows us to choose what our consciousness is ultimately attracted to.

Our universe is governed by the laws of attraction, and we attract the same energy we give off. Although evil is a part of this universe, it was not intended, and one day our universe will come to an end, and all evil will be demolished. God will make a new universe in which all dimensions will coalesce in harmony with a new heaven and earth where love will last an eternity, and no one will suffer eternal death.

What I learned from God when I was enveloped in his omnipotent presence was the amount of love he has for each one of us, and each of us is a part of God and we are all a part of each other. I realized that Jesus comes to those who are ready to accept him, but that may not happen for some people until after they die, because we don't really die, we just leave our mortal bodies.

Our earthly life is a journey in which we choose to grow in love and have a relationship with our creator, but everyone is on their own timeline. Every tribulation we encounter teaches us a lesson in which we can learn from, and at some point in our lives, every one of us we will be faced with the questions of who are we, who do we want to be and, where are we going?

Who Are We

Before we came to Earth, we were all a part of creation, and we watched our Father create, as we lingered in the heavens in our spirit form of LOVE. We came to Earth to embody our true selves and to share our love with each other, and our consciousness of who we are lies deep within our soul.

What is consciousness and how does it work in our brain? Neuroscientists are baffled by the complexity of our brain in how it operates. Francis Crick, a neuroscientist, was working on a paper just days before his death and his findings suggested our consciousness needs something like an orchestra conductor to bind all of our external and internal perceptions together.

After my experience, I realized what God had shown me was the many facets and intriguing capacity of the brain, not just the brain itself, but the mystery component that operates the brain.

God took me through different parts of my consciousness, and I reached a high level of consciousness in which I was able to speak to him directly through thought.

Although I am unable to reach this capacity today, I was given a gift for a brief period of time, in which a veil was lifted and I was able to access a dimension that exists right in front of our very eyes but that we cannot see.

The intriguing part of our universe is the dominating force that controls the expansion of it, which is dark energy. Astronomers have given dark energy its name due to the fact that it is an unknown agent that they cannot explain. However, it is the same phenomenon that we encounter when neuroscientists are baffled by the unknown force that controls our brain.

I realized after my experience that God is a part of our consciousness and we are a part of God's consciousness, which makes up our universe. We are in fact living in a cosmic consciousness and that is why everything and everyone is connected, and our thoughts are the most important fundamental in our relationship with our creator.

Our spirit is linked to this dominating force—this is why I believe, when we pass on, we are able to bring our memories and our personalities along with us.

Who are we, and are we a reflection of ourselves or others? We get to know who we are by how others see us, and we find our identity by where we live, our race, gender, apparel, occupation, beliefs, and our past experiences.

We find something new about ourselves the moment we step outside our comfort zone and when we surround ourselves with other people. But are we learning new things about ourselves or others?

I used to have a hard time knowing who I truly was, because I always felt different depending who I was with—whether I was with my family, friends, children, coworkers, or strangers.

I sometimes didn't like who I was when certain people were around, because I felt as though they brought out certain traits in myself I didn't like.

What I didn't realize is that we only mirror others by how we feel about ourselves. The real question is, are we who we think we are?

We know we are all different, but maybe not in the way we think. Most of the time, the things we don't like about other people are what we don't like about ourselves.

I always find myself butting heads with my son, because he's very opinionated, and I get frustrated when he doesn't listen. I feel like sometimes I'm battling myself, and although we are different, we are a lot alike.

We are so busy comparing ourselves to others that we forget to see people through God's eyes. But what if we were able to?

Our journey here leads us to knowing who we are, to losing ourselves, then back to remembering who we once were. It leads us all to the same place. A place where we all long for love and acceptance, just like a child. Our innocence gave us clarity and defined our purpose in life.

At one time in our lives we were all carefree and innocent before the world. What changed? Aren't we all children at heart?

God designed us, and we developed our personality, before we ever lost our way. What did we lose? We lost our innocence, and we picked up worldly habits along the way.

I remember when I was a child, I would walk up to another child at recess and ask them if they wanted to be my friend. Why can't life be that simple, and why can't we go back to reaching out to others without fear?

When we were children, most of us were not concerned with what other kids were wearing, or what their beliefs were on politics or religion. We saw other children as equals, and we talked to them with an open mind, heart, and soul.

Although some children were mean to us, and hurt our feelings, we learned soon enough that it was not our fault for how they treated us. Our reliance kept us going, and we never lost the desire to make new friends and forgive others.

Most of us now have gotten married and have families of our own, but we have isolated ourselves from other families because of our differences. How do we return to innocence and regain what we have lost? Our Heavenly

Father wants us to seek him for this very reason.

This vulnerability is hard to reach when we think we have it all figured out. Our stubbornness causes us to put up a wall between God and others.

We are never too old to cry out to God like a child, because deep within all of us is our childlike nature that we have forgotten—it lies deep within our subconscious.

Let's remember who we once were by allowing our Heavenly Father to show us. If we look at others and try to see the child hiding underneath, we can learn to love people and find the good in them.

We can inspire others by our innocent nature, and in time, we can let go of the world and hold on to our true selves and embrace one another for all time.

Gift of Time

When I feel like I'm running out of time, I always think of the song, *Vienna*, by Billy Joel. When I listen to it, I can't help but get emotional, because I know that I'm guilty of spreading myself too thin, and sometimes I forget to ask God for guidance. There are so many things I want to do, but I always feel there's never enough time to get everything done. I have to stop and remind myself that Jesus waits for us to call on him, and although there are many things we want to achieve, we can't do everything and that's okay. When we are too busy, we end up missing precious moments with our family and friends and are unable to see those around us.

In our fast-paced environment, we are always on the run and seem to take every minute focusing on the next thing we have to do. How can we stop our minds from wandering and instead allow our minds to rest in the present moment?

I remember one day I was rocking my daughter to sleep. While I was rocking her, my mind was already focused on putting the clothes in the dryer. The energy I was giving off was a sense of urgency, and this was causing her to be fussy. I stopped and gazed into her sleepy eyes and thought to myself how much I loved her and started singing her lullaby in a softer tone. I kept my thoughts focused on that very moment, taking it all in and letting myself enjoy the stillness. The light outside reflecting off of her bright blue eyes, her beautiful soft skin, and the pure innocence radiating from her soul. And before I knew it, she was sound asleep.

All we have are moments with each other, and we must practice being present in each moment so we can learn to appreciate each other.

We are limited through our daily lives, because we are constricted by time. How do we set time aside for other people? The question is, are we truly managing our time? Is each minute of our day accounted for? What if we used each minute of our day the way God wanted us to?

Imagine waking up every morning being thankful and asking God to use us to help others. Asking God to give us His compassion and fill us up with His love.

We could walk into our local coffee shop and our attitude would be different. We would order our usual cup of coffee, but this time we could ask the person working how they are doing and really mean it. The next time we walked in, we could call them by their name and ask them how their weekend went. We could drive past a homeless person and see them with different eyes. We could go to work and see our coworkers as family members and not just other employees. We could learn to work as a team, instead of viewing others as our competitors.

We could spend each minute of our day spreading love and encouragement to one another rather than squandering our time with life's constant busyness. Love is contagious and it can spread like wildfire. If we affect one person and they go on to affect someone else, so it continues on until it triggers a domino effect.

We could stand united, and the ones who remained selfish would be recognized for who they were. We would be able to discern between good and evil, and in time, it would not matter what our opinions were on politics or religion, we could learn to love one another. If we prayed for God to give us His compassion, we could help others through our true intentions instead of passing judgement and forcing fake smiles.

We could pray for God to guide our every thought, so we could live in constant companionship with Him. We must understand that to have that kind of love and compassion for others, we must pray for it.

Why are we praying for God to intervene when He already has? He already lived a human life through Jesus. He died for us, and then gave us His spirit that lives in each one of us, so why do we keep asking Him to help when it's up to us? Jesus told us to spread the good news to the ends of the earth and then He would return. What does that mean? Are we supposed to go out and forcefully talk to people about God? Or are we supposed to live how God wants us to and show others through our actions?

To be a reflection of Jesus, we must change the way we are living and focus on bringing our family close. We can do this by being the change and leading by example. Then we can show others around us by making personal relationships with one person at a time. Developing trust with that person, showing them through small acts of kindness. In time, that person may or may not be affected, but we have at least affected them in some way by showing them what it means to be a true disciple.

As the years pass by, we always ask ourselves, where did the time go? The question we should ask is whether we are using time as a gift or abusing the gift of time.

We will all eventually leave this plane of existence, and when that day comes, we will have to sit in front of God and give an account for our lives. How did we spend the time He gave us? Did we use our time here on Earth the way He intended?

God laid out our lives before we were ever born—He designed us with intention, love, and purpose.

Each one of us has a mission in this life. Our lives are full of choices, and each decision we make leads us down a different path.

We have the choice to be healthier, travel, make new friends, or start a new career. Our decisions not only impact our lives, but also the lives of those around us, and one wrong decision we make can even cost someone their life.

When I was younger, I had a vivid imagination, but I was very impatient, so I didn't enjoy reading. The only books I read were the ones in which you could choose your own adventure. On each page it would give you a choice at the bottom, and the ending would be different based on the choice you made.

God sees our lives as a series of choices and different outcomes, and although it's more complex than a storybook, we must understand that we create our destiny. But God gives us many opportunities to live a better life, no matter what path we are on.

In the movie *Forrest Gump,* I always took comfort in the way he lived his life, going through life like a feather floating free from time. He didn't worry about his future, and he was able to stay in the present moment and take in all of the opportunities that life presented to him. When he ran across the country, he inspired many people along the way—he gave people hope. When others asked his purpose for running, he simply stated, "I just felt like running."

Life presents itself to us, and although we choose what we want to do, there is always a strange coincidence that finds us reflecting back as to why we didn't take that job, or answer that phone call, and what our lives would be like if we had.

How can we follow our dreams while living in the present moment? What are dreams? Dreams are our hope for our future, and hope is our weapon against fear and worry.

One of my favorite quotes by Walt Disney is, "A dream is a wish your heart makes." When we plan for our future, we should be excited, because if our heart is truly guiding us, then we should feel a sense of comfort in knowing we will accomplish what has been promised to us. The moment we give into fear or worry, we will hinder our full potential to accomplish our goals.

Before I started my business, I had a vision of the end result in my mind. In order to keep myself on track, without getting discouraged, I made a list of each step and crossed them off as I accomplished them. There were some days when I couldn't do anything but have hope, and I started to get discouraged because my plan was taking longer than I expected. It took three years to finally open my business. My first opening failed, and it took a huge emotional and financial toll on my family. I ended up opening my business again after moving back to my hometown, and now I am living the dream I had envisioned five years ago. I realized that I had rushed God's plan because I lacked patience. If I had waited on God's timing, I would not have endured so much failure and pain.

How do we live in the present moment while planning for our future? Patience is key in understanding God's ways. When we are impatient, it's because we are too focused on the future, and we aren't appreciating the present moment. We know the steps it takes to accomplish our goals, but we should also trust in God's timing for each goal and not rush them. When we allow our minds to stay focused on the present moment, we will be more aware of the many signs leading us in the right direction.

That does not mean failure is bad and should be avoided. We are expected to make mistakes, because that's in our human nature. Our mistakes help shape our future, so we reach our goals more humbly. If we acquire everything too easily, we will not appreciate what we have.

Sometimes God has better plans for our future, and when we think we have our future plans set, a huge curveball gets thrown at us that changes the course of our lives. This is why God gave us hope.

Hope

One of my favorite movies is *The Shawshank Redemption.* The main character, Andy, finds himself in prison, serving a life sentence for a crime he didn't commit. He explained that his reason for his sanity was hope.

His friend, Red, told him, "Hope is a dangerous thing, my friend. It can kill a man." Andy replied, "Then I guess it comes down to a single choice. Get busy living or get busy dying."

Andy was determined to get out of prison, and he did. In a letter to Red, he wrote, "Remember, Red, hope is a good thing, maybe the best of things, and no good thing ever dies."

God never wants us to give up hope, even in our most dire circumstances. There is a saying that states, "There's always light at the end of the tunnel," and that is true for us all. We have a living God, and He does not live in our past or future, but in our present moment, through us, through our universe, and our hope lies within Him.

Why do we get our hopes up? As we know, God created hope for us as a reminder that we have as many chances as we need in order to figure out our mission in life. Shouldn't we give everyone else the same leniency God grants us?

Expectations cause us to be unsatisfied because we expect too much and give too little. We expect a lot from our children, spouses, parents, and friends. How can we grow in love if we have expectations? We must replace expectations with appreciation.

Before I had my experience, I had very strong religious beliefs. My beliefs were so strong, I expected my husband to think the same way I did. I wanted him to love Jesus, and I kept thinking that if he didn't, he was not going to heaven. I kept pressuring him, and my expectations were only pushing him further away from knowing Jesus.

We expect everyone in our lives should at some point accept our beliefs, but we are only pushing them further away. If we learn to appreciate and accept others as they are, we can show them the light that shines within us. Our light is what makes others gravitate toward us.

That does not mean we need to put ourselves around those who hurt us, but instead let those come to us that need us. Those who want to change follow strong leaders, not judgers and scorners.

Turning the other cheek is the hardest part in our daily interactions, because we must learn to be the bigger person in situations that cause us anger. Once we give into anger, we are unable to stay in connection with our true selves, and our judgement becomes cloudy.

We must learn to walk away and collect our thoughts, so we can ask God to help us.

In order to spread love, we need to love ourselves first. We do not have to take abuse from others, but instead we should not be afraid to tell others how we truly feel. Growing in love also means expressing our emotions, so we can teach others how to grow as well, as long as we approach each situation with grace.

I sometimes have a difficult time disciplining my son. I get trapped in the notion that I need to remain disappointed by the bad decisions he makes.

When he would apologize, I would ask him, "What's the point in apologizing if you're just going to do it again?" My expectations for him far exceeded his ability to live up to my standards. I wasn't excepting his apology, because I was upset that he kept making the same mistakes.

How could I expect him to promise me that he wasn't going to make another mistake? As hard as we try, we are always going to make mistakes. We need to recognize that our children are not any different than we are. Refusing my son's apology only caused him to feel shame, and as a result, that only caused more division between us.

For every mistake we make there is always a consequence—everything we do has an effect. Disciplining our children should be that simple. Whether the consequence is doing yard work or taking TV away that week. They can pay the consequence, but in the meantime, we don't have to stop loving them, and we don't have to get angry and hold a grudge.

Since we do not have to earn God's love, we also need to remember that our children do not have to earn our love, because our love should be unconditional.

Our mistakes cause us to learn and grow. Some of us make the same mistake more than once, but eventually we always have to face the consequences of our mistakes and hopefully that will make us want to change our ways.

How do we get our children to listen to us? Patience is key in understanding what our children need. We should learn to assess the situation and ask God for his love and understanding before we let our emotions cloud our judgement.

Learning who our Heavenly Father is equips us with the ability to handle situations in a godly manner, so we are able to teach our children how He teaches us. He is slow to anger and His patience far exceeds our understanding.

Leading by example is the most important aspect in parenting. Our children look up to us—we need to be the best role models, so they can learn from us. If we expect our children to have a clean room every day, then we too must have a clean room. If we expect our children to be humble, then we too need to display a humble attitude toward others. Although this takes discipline and effort on our part, being the best we can be will also benefit our children.

Being a parent does not mean that we need to teach our children that we are always right. Admitting our faults encourages our children to admit their faults. If they see us taking accountability for our actions, they will learn to not carry a prideful burden throughout their life.

Our Heavenly Father never gives up on any of us and always has hope that we will eventually ask him for guidance. He would never shame or abandon any of us regardless of our actions. We should never give up on any of our children and never lose faith that they will find their way. Our children are supposed to be a reflection of us, and in order to raise them properly, we should try to be a reflection of our Heavenly Father

Burdens

Deep in our subconscious are burdens passed down to us from our past.

Holding a grudge and guilt are huge burdens most of us carry by not forgiving ourselves for something we did in our past or not forgiving others. These burdens cause us to trap our emotions, and the negativity separates us from accepting God's love and loving others.

How can we let go of something that we can't see? It's simple. We must pray to God to forgive us, and pray to help us forgive the ones who hurt us. Prayer can be powerful if we truly believe that God can heal our broken hearts.

There were many people in my past that I held grudges against, but I have forgiven them. Forgiving someone doesn't always mean that you have to call them up and tell them you forgive them. It is just making peace with that person in your heart, freeing yourself from the trapped anger and handing it over to God.

There are many burdens in this world like fear, worry, shame, jealousy, greed, lust, power, pride, and many more that cause divide. All of these burdens get passed on from one person to the next through our interactions.

Someone does something to hurt us, and in retaliation we hurt someone else to pass on the burden, so we can release the anger we feel. We may not be able to recall a time this has happened, but we have all done it.

How can we break the chain and learn to love each other? How can we let go of the past and truly forgive someone? We don't have to pass burdens on to each other when we can give them to God.

I moved away from hometown in my early twenties, and after ten years, my husband and I moved back to my hometown to be near my family. My mom and I never had a close relationship, and we were trying to get to know each other.

We ended up getting into a huge argument, and the past was brought up. It ended up causing a lot of pent up emotions to come out in a very negative way. I didn't speak to my mom for over two months. I had a hard time getting over some of the things that we said to each other. I didn't think I was in the wrong, and I thought that she owed me an apology—I'm sure she felt the same way I did.

I realized that I needed to let go of the past and my pride so that I could allow myself to love my mother. We all have the choice to change who we are, and we can decide to grow in love or stay trapped in the past. God can heal any burden we carry deep within us, as long as we can allow ourselves to realize what those burdens are and surrender to His will.

We don't have the right to judge someone for wronging us, because we too have wronged others in our lives, whether we realize it or not. In order to break the vicious cycle, we need to accept that we are not perfect.

We are all broken in some way, and we all carry burdens. In order to heal our burdens, we need to reveal our scars to one another, open up our hearts without fear, and accept others' hearts without judgement.

What language are we speaking to each other? As we know, we are all made of energy which is why we can connect to nature and to others without expressing words. Our thoughts are made of energy. What we think affects our mood, and the vibration we give off in the form of energy affects those around us.

Have you ever walked into a room and felt emotions from others that altered your mood? Are there some people that you feel at peace with and you love being around them?

We are emotional beings, and although we may try to hide what we are feeling by our outward appearance, that does not change what energy we are giving off to others.

Someone can say they are a follower of God, but you either feel loved by that person or you feel negativity. Why is this? What is this person thinking about? Is it you, or is it them?

People walk around with burdens they carry deep within their subconscious. They carry these burdens unaware, and as a result, their thought process conforms around the way they feel about themselves.

When I was little, I could never figure out why other kids hated me. It was disappointing when I would show someone my feelings and they would reject me. I remember always trying to make friends, but I had a very hard time getting other kids to accept me.

This was a constant pattern throughout my life growing up, but I never wanted to give up on anyone, because I always saw the good in people, despite the ugliness they portrayed. Many times I forgave people, but they would see that as a sign of weakness and walk all over me. The few friends I did have, I always feared they were going to wake up one day and realize I wasn't good enough and stop speaking to me.

I'm not sure why I felt so worthless, but today I can look back at the broken girl that I once was and rest assured knowing that God healed my broken heart and took away my burden of shame buried deep within.

What I didn't realize is that the person I thought I was, I wasn't. I had to come to a point in my life and accept myself. The only way I was able to do this was when I allowed myself to accept God's love. The acceptance I was searching for was His, and He was with me the whole time.

God's language is love. If we are truly connected to our creator, then we are able to accept his love, and in return we can give that love to others.

The question again is, what language are we speaking to others? Are we able to lift someone's spirit with our love? Are we emotionally strong enough to do so? The first step is healing the burdens we carry deep within, by reaching out to God and searching our whole heart until we reach a state of complete humiliation.

If we are going to claim "God" in our lives, we should aim to be in constant connection with Him, so we can raise the state of our vibration. If we are giving off a vibration of love, we can send it to people all around us. We will also be sensitive to negative energy vibrations, and we can use this gift to help protect our loved ones from evil in this world.

Language barriers and other religions are not what separate us from each other—it's our energy, and the choice to accept God's love, let go of our burdens, and love others how He does.

Gifts

After graduating culinary school, I spent many years going from one job to the next. I remember how I felt after graduating, and since I had made it to the top of my class, I had gained a sense of pride. I carried that pride with me into my career, which hindered my learning experience.

I spent many years thinking I would never amount to anything, and when I finally accomplished something, I didn't want anyone standing in my way. What I didn't realize at the time was my pride was getting in the way of my growth. I never wanted to admit my faults, and I was too prideful to take anyone else's advice. Eventually my pride led me down a dark path until it cost me my job.

Pride is one of the worst burdens some of us carry in life. It hinders our ability to learn from others, because we think we have it all figured out.

Although it's great to feel a sense of pride after accomplishing our goals, we should always humble ourselves, and thank the Lord for giving us the ability and perseverance to achieve them.

Each one of us has special gifts that we were born with, and just like there is not one snowflake alike, we are all unique and designed with special talents. We are not expected to know everything, and not one person can. We are supposed to share our gifts with each other, so we can all grow and become one large family.

We do not need to be jealous or envious of others for their gifts—we each have our own. What gift has God given us and are we using it? If we are not using our gifts, then we are not expressing ourselves and we are not able to share with others.

Whether we are good at writing, drawing, painting, or singing, we need to use our gifts as a positive outlet to ignite our soul, all the while focusing on being humble and gracious and learning from others around us. If our intent is to honor our Father and inspire others, then our expression will come from our heart instead of our pride.

In the process of writing this book, I thank God every day for giving me the ability to write, and I know He is speaking to me through my writing. I also know He speaks to others through their gifts, whether it's writing, music, art, or public speaking.

The most important lesson I learned from God was humbling myself, when I was gifted with his knowledge

God reminded me that each of us plays a vital role in contribution to his plan, and knowledge is a gift, but desiring to know everything does not come from God.

We can all learn from each other and share our gifts, so we can connect to God and connect to each other by letting go of our pride, opening our hearts, and expressing our love.

Within all of us is the gift of the Holy Spirit that redeems us. It is a gift that must be accepted with gratitude. Like all gifts, if we do not use it, it will be left in an unopened box to be forgotten. In order to open the box, we must open our heart, mind, and soul and allow the Holy Spirit to work through us.

We are given so many gifts, and God sees us for the people He created us to be. He looks past the mistakes and sees us in all of His glory.

In order to get over the wall that divides us from being the person we were created to be, we must think positively and focus on the good in ourselves. We must embrace the gifts we are given and focus only on the good in others.

While there is a dark cloud lingering over many people in this world, we can show them the light by inspiring them to be better through our talents and actions. We will be so busy making ourselves better, in the process we will make those around us better for it.

Each day is a gift, and we must wake up and rejoice that we have another day to help make a difference in this world.

What can we do today to make ourselves better for God? What small step can we take to help achieve our goals, so we can fulfill the destiny God has called us to do?

In order to see the pages God has written in our book, we must believe in ourselves. We must envision the dream in our hearts so we can find the missing pages in our lives. When we use our imagination and visualize our future selves living out our full potential, we are manifesting a pathway. Then each day we can take another step toward our dreams, so we can wake up one day into our new reality.

God shows us what He's calling us to do—the signs are all around us. Through people we meet, what we are reading, seeing, or hearing—as long as we are paying attention.

Since we were created from God's dream, He is connected to everything and everyone, so He can influence others to help us along the way.

We cannot help others unless we first help ourselves. We must fulfill our destiny so that we can help others fulfill theirs.

I remember there were moments in my life when my heart wasn't in something I was doing, and I did not have ambition. God gives us many clues as to why we feel the way we do, because He's a part of our consciousness.

Some people say they don't have God in their lives, and although they may not acknowledge

God, or have a relationship with him, everyone still has a conscious.

What is a conscious? In the movie *Pinocchio,* it was a small cricket named Jiminy that told Pinocchio right from wrong. He didn't always listen to his conscious, and when he didn't, he got himself into trouble.

Our conscious is God, and although we cannot hear him, we can feel when we are making the right choices in our lives by trusting our instincts.

How is it possible for people to spend their life hurting others, if they too have a conscious? The longer we go down our own path against God's will, the more we distance ourselves from God.

Take addiction, for example. Although we know it is not right to become reliant on drugs or alcohol, the longer we use substances, the more accustomed we become to them, and the feeling of it being wrong starts to fade as it becomes a part of our daily lives.

We are accustomed to many sins in which we are unaware of, because our society forces us to adapt to our surroundings. Some people grow up in an environment in which they are forced to live a life based on their culture, but it is not their fault for what they have grown accustomed to.

Although we are limited by our circumstances, we can still choose to connect to our Creator and live our lives with a different mindset. What better mindset than through Jesus?

Who is Jesus, and what gift has He given all of humanity? When Jesus lived a human life on Earth, He wanted to bring peace to everyone. He was not concerned by religious rules—his concern was bringing everyone together through God's love. He did not conform to his society, but instead he led his disciples through a path less traveled for the good of humanity.

Anyone who is seeking God will find Jesus, because Jesus is God's gift to us all. God lives within Jesus, and the Holy Spirit lives inside every one of us.

Every religion that practices love has meaning and is a stepping stone to God. It is not our mission to judge others for their beliefs or try to change them, but only to accept them for who they are, so we can all grow in love.

Jesus Christ is my Savior, but He didn't want us roaming the earth, forcing others to accept our beliefs. He wanted us to spread the good news by spreading His love.

My constant prayer to God is for Him to continue to fill me with His love daily, so that I can give it to others. It is my mission, and in the process, I will continue to write what I have learned throughout my journey.

My inspiration comes from the amount of love that I felt from God the moment I met him. I sought God out, and I found a loving father and mother.

I was able to see a glimpse into our Creator's eyes and see how much love He has for everyone. I will never forget that moment, and it will never fade. I pray that others can experience a glimpse into heaven as I did.

God's gift of eternal life is paid in full by His sacrifice—Jesus was willing to fulfill this mission and He did, and there is nothing to worry about or fear.

What does it mean when someone claims to be saved by Jesus? Some ask, how could a man save us from sin? People question whether or not Jesus did in fact live a sinless life. How could He possibly live a sinless life in a fallen world? I too pondered these questions before my experience.

God taught me that we are all born with sin, because sin was passed down to us from many generations. The question is, how was Jesus different? Since Jesus was conceived through the Holy Spirit and was born of a virgin, He was born free from sin, and God was able to live a human life through His Son. Jesus did not have burdens that were passed down to him from generations; therefore, He was able to bear our burdens.

We too were sent to Earth for our own mission, but we have forgotten about who we were before we came to Earth. Jesus did not forget why He was sent to Earth, and He knew His mission.

What does it mean to be saved and born again? Does this mean we won't sin after our rebirth? After I had accepted Jesus as my savior, I felt free, but I wasn't free from sin. My soul no longer felt trapped by the world, and I knew my rebirth would be when I left this life and went home.

Although some of us get to experience a sense of what it feels like to be set free, we only get a brief moment in which we feel free from our burdens until sin enters back into our consciousness. We will consciously try to live a godly life, but we will always fall short. Our freedom is our faith in knowing our spirit is set free and knowing where our true home is. For others that have different beliefs, they might experience something similar as being saved, but they too have been touched by the Holy Spirit within them, without realizing it. It's a choice to find God within us, to have a relationship with our Creator, and to have the desire and a heart that yearns for love.

When someone asks me what my religion is and what denomination I belong to, I say that my religion is LOVE, I belong to God, but my journey is finding my way to live through Jesus each day.

Although religion is a stepping stone to our Father, we should stay away from teachings that cause us to fear. Fear that we cannot make mistakes, fear that we have lost God, fear that we will be led astray by other beliefs, fear of karma, fear that the end is coming and we will be left behind, and fear of eternal death.

After reading many books and hearing many testimonies of people who had a near death experience, they all experienced the same thing I did—LOVE. Although some experienced going to a place without love, they were always rescued out of the darkness when they cried out to God.

The deception behind religion was created by the enemy, because the enemy is FEAR.

To follow Jesus, we must think like Him. We must not worry about others by thinking they are lost because of their beliefs. Worry and fear are very close at hand, and one of the enemy's tricks is to divide us from what Jesus values most, which is to love one another. We can't learn to love others if we can't accept them as they are.

Most of us know the Ten Commandments, and while most of us acknowledge them and live by them, we have forgotten the main one—to love thy neighbor as thyself.

When Jesus was asked by His disciple, Mathew, about upholding the Ten Commandments, Jesus said, "Owe no man anything, but to love one another: for he that loveth another hath fulfilled the law."

There are some Christian pastors that still read from the Old Testament and instill fear upon people and teach hate, by adhering to religious rules and regulations. They teach that we must listen to only their teachings, because they are right and everyone else is wrong.

To read the Old Testament is not wrong of us, but we must not take the context so literally, by using it as a weapon against others.

Jesus said, "Obedience must be from the heart (attitudes and intentions) rather than just technical observance of the letter of the law." Attitudes and intentions are created through our thought patterns, and we must start there.

There are some Christian churches that have drastically changed over time, and they teach love and acceptance. But going to church is not required of us, and we must not think that just because we don't go to church, we are unworthy of God's love.

I have found more peace reading my Bible, sitting in my favorite chair by the window, and listening to the sounds of nature outside, and in doing so, I am able to hear God more clearly. One of my favorite Bible quotes is, "Be still and know that I am God."

To know Jesus is to find our inner peace and to become one with God, and we will have freedom from the deception religion has created.

Serving God just means being thankful for the gifts He has given us and embracing each day positively, because our Heavenly Father just wants what all parents want, which is for us all to be happy.

Quantum World

What is quantum theory, and does it go against what religion has taught us? We are living at an age in which we can study subatomic particles on a microscopic level due to our advancements in technology.

Our advancements have given us more insight into what we are all made of and the opportunity to observe matter itself.

Before I became a follower of Christ, I was very fascinated by quantum theory and read many books on the topic. Of course, I cannot understand physics, so my comprehension was very limited. Yet, I was still intrigued by the concept, and my curiosity was the very basis that lead me down this path.

Groundbreaking research has revealed that atoms can be in two places at one time. Physicists have conducted this study by observing microscopic particles, and they concluded that objects of the quantum world do not move along a single, well-defined path. Rather, they can simultaneously take different paths and end up at different places at once, and pop in and out of plain sight.

How is it possible for atoms to follow their own rules, but we are limited and confined to the laws that govern our universe, even though we are made of energy?

After Jesus' resurrection, He appeared to His disciples many times in human form, but He was able to vanish in and out of plain sight, which defies the laws of our space time dimension. He told His disciples many times that His kingdom was not a part of this world, and He was going to prepare a place for us all.

Reading these stories, it seems impossible for a man to vanish and be in more than one place at one time, but not for God.

God is not confined to this universe as we are, and as quantum studies have proven, matter itself can vanish in and out of our time dimension.

God expected us to make new discoveries and technological advancements so that we could learn and grow. He expected us to incorporate what we have learned in science into our religious beliefs because, after all, everything is God's creation.

The Holy Bible is the basis for our understanding in knowing who God is, and it is full of stories of tribulations and God's divine interventions, yet there are many miraculous testimonies from all throughout history since the Bible was written. In the present moment, our fast-paced society is drastically different from biblical times, and although we are no longer living a simple life, God has not abandoned us.

God expected us to connect the dots and use our knowledge as well as keep an open mind when it comes to science. Some scientists are ignorant to religion, as some religious leaders are ignorant to science, but it does not have to be that way if we work together and create a better understanding for all of humanity.

What I encountered during my experience was different than any of the other near death experiences I read. Before I got sick and had my brush with death, I had a spiritual awakening and saw many visions. I saw future events that may or may not take place. I realized that since my consciousness was in a place without time, I was able to see possible future events, but God helped me understand that they would not take place unless I chose those paths.

When I looked up studies on quantum theory, I was able to understand how this was possible based on the studies that were conducted. In one of my visions, I saw that God had not meant for evil to get into the world, so I was able to interpret the Bible differently, as I saw His plan for all of humanity flash before my eyes.

In my vision, I saw that in the Garden of Eden, God had created a small piece of heaven on Earth free from sin. He created this place to protect His children, to keep them close to Him, away from the evil that entered the world.

Adam and Eve had no burdens that separated them from each other or from God, so during that time, they could freely speak to each other telepathically and could hear God clearly.

God gave them guidance and told them not to listen to anyone but Him and that He would provide everything they needed. They took it upon themselves to disobey and go their own way, thinking they knew better than God. In doing so, this caused them to run away from God, ashamed. The longer they went down their own path, the more burdens they caused (as consequences of sin).

In time, many burdens were passed down from one generation to the next, until God was unable to connect to man.

God intervened many times throughout history to help people and show them signs. Over time, our world became a product of sin, and we were living a way God had not intended for us to live, but He knew the ultimate path we could possibly go down, so He sent Jesus.

God lived a human life through His Son Jesus, teaching others how we are supposed to live. To love one another and Him, and to teach others this important fundamental.

People ask, "If God loves us, why would he allow suffering or evil?" I too used to wonder this before God revealed himself to me.

Many claim that God created evil so we would have free will, but evil is not a part of God, because GOD is LOVE. He created everything with His perfect love, and His desire was for love to flourish.

God gave us free will, because He wanted us to have the ability to think for ourselves. He can see many paths that we may possibly choose, but He cannot see what path we will choose until we have made a choice. Once He granted us free will, He gave up the power to control our outcomes, and therefore, He waits on us.

He also gave his angels free will, and that is why He had to create a plan to save us after his angels had already made their choice. The enemy was one of God's angels, and this evil resides in a dimension separate from God. Although we cannot see these dimensions, they are very close to us, and angels can cross over into our time dimension and can influence us in many ways.

God created our universe outside of creation, but within our universe is God's loving consciousness because He created everything through thought. God is also a part of our consciousness, and when we align our thoughts with God, He is able to bring blessings into our lives. He designed our universe in this manner so we could stay in constant connection to Him.

God created us in His image, and we truly can be a reflection of Him if we maintain our connection and pray without ceasing.

Prayers

How are we praying and how can we expect our prayers to be answered without faith?

Some of us who pray usually do it right before bed, as we drift off to sleep. The same redundant prayer that keeps us in what we feel is "good graces" with our Lord, but why do we feel prayers should be forced instead of a part of who we are?

As we know, God is a part of our consciousness and lives through us, so what's keeping us from living through Him?

We don't need to pray at certain times if we always acknowledge God's presence and keep Him in line with our thoughts. We don't need to be afraid of what we think, or fear prayer, but rather should feel the opposite. We should be happy we have someone to talk to that knows us better than we know ourselves.

The enemy tries to trick us all the time by sending dark thoughts into our mind. It can be thoughts about our past, worries for the future, or our insecurities. Those thoughts can travel right past us if we hold on to God instead of holding those thoughts captive. We also don't need to feel ashamed, because our Father knows our hearts and does not blame us for the sin in the world.

Before my experience, I never really prayed because I would always worry. What I realized is that God cannot bless us if we don't trust him, and even though I prayed, I doubted God by worrying, so my prayers were meaningless.

In the movie *Peter Pan*, when he was teaching the kids in the nursery how to fly, he said, "All you need is faith and trust, and a little bit of pixie dust."

Our faith and trust in God gives him the ability to work blessings into our lives, and He provides the pixie dust so we can overcome any obstacle and reach any goal within our hearts.

Prayers are very personal, and although it's great to be a part of a church and pray among others, we should not pray to look pleasing to others, or by telling others we are praying for them. We are not the ones who deserve the credit, because God works through us.

Keeping God in our thoughts is a constant, but real prayer is sacred and is best practiced when no one is looking. When we are alone, we are able to connect to God spiritually—our spirits become free when we are not being observed by others.

Praying for others is a selfless act if God is our only witness, and if we pray for others with true compassion, it will come from our hearts and can reach God's heart.

Before I got to know God, I used to have a hard time praying, because I thought I was being selfish, and thought why would God answer my prayers when He has the whole world to worry about?

We are all made of energy, and while our earthly bodies keep us confined to our earthly realm, our thoughts are not confined to our space time dimension. When we pray, our thoughts can reach our Heavenly Father who is in a realm outside of time. He is able to hear us, and he can spend any amount of time needed to answer our prayers.

He works in his own ways and knows the best time in our lives when our prayers should be answered. We must trust God is not ignoring us, but preparing our blessings in advance.

Since our thoughts reach our Heavenly Father, we can talk to God anytime we want through our mind. Meditation can be practiced to help calm our minds. By clearing our mind and focusing on the stillness of the ocean breeze, or the sound of the rain, we are able to hear God more clearly.

We may not hear a voice, but we will have thoughts come to us that we can identify more easily if we stop our minds from racing.

We are all children of God, we are LOVE, and we need to always remind ourselves of that by constantly battling the enemy with our positive thoughts. God has us in the palm of His hand, and nothing can take us away from Him because we belong to Him.

Worship can be done in many ways, like singing to positive music, dancing, laughing, being in tune with nature, and just being thankful. Worship is a powerful way to connect to God and keeps us in line with Him, so we can keep our mind and bodies healthy.

If we are always in line with God through our thought process, we will display Godly characteristics, because our thoughts make us who we are, and we can show others who God is through our actions.

Some people believe that God is just a bystander watching from afar, not doing anything, just like an ant bully with a magnifying glass. But that is not true. God created us in His image. He feels the same emotions we do, and He feels them at the same time we are feeling them. He sees and feels the pain in the world, but He also sees and feels the joy and laughter.

There are times when I become too serious, and I let what's going on in the world affect me. I feel as though I should not be allowed to have fun while others are suffering in the world. I have to remind myself that God has a relationship with each one of us, whether we acknowledge Him or not. He is in an eternal place looking in, and inside each one of us— he's along for the ride and wants us to be happy.

He created man and woman in His likeness, which means He can relate to us all because He has the same traits men and women have combined.

He is slow to anger, and although He is very patient, He still gets upset with the enemy who uses His children to hurt others. He has to feel the anguish, disappointment, and the pain. He has a plan for each one of us, and it's all a part of a master plan that we could never possibly comprehend.

Sometimes I don't understand why innocent lives are taken and I question God. Why did He let that happen? I try to put myself in God's shoes, which are pretty big shoes, but I try to imagine what it would be like to have to decide which one of my children I would want to save. The answer is simple: all of them.

God may see all possible future outcomes for each one of us, and maybe He brings some of us home early to save us from a life of suffering.

He also has to endure the pain of seeing His children mourn for the loss of their loved ones, which must be very hard for Him since some of us get mad at God because we don't understand His ways.

What are we missing? It's plain and simple— we are not trusting God. When we are teaching our children, they always ask us why, and the answer is always the same: "Because I know what's best for you." Sometimes our children hate us for it, but that's a sacrifice we have to make in order to protect them. God is just trying to save all of us, and He's never going to give up, even if it means having to endure more pain so He can fulfill the ultimate destiny He has for all of humanity.

We hear stories of miracles happening when someone beats death with all odds against them, or a healthy person suddenly dies when doctors did everything they could to save them. Some people cross over and meet God and Jesus, and they come back to tell their story.

We are now living in an age where it is possible to hear these miraculous testimonies from others due to our technology. Although technology has created a divide in some instances, it has also helped us connect to the world around us, so we are able to see the many proofs of God's handiwork.

It's all a part of God's plan, as long as we use it for good. By connecting to those around us, it helps us all understand His master plan for humanity, but most importantly, it helps us trust his timing.

Technology

When I was little, I played outside a lot and I always looked for bugs to catch. I remember I would step on an ant and I would watch the other ants carry their injured friend back to their nest.

Ant colonies actually work together as a team—they don't have a leader, they all just have specific duties they were designed to do by instinct.

One ant could not survive if I took it away from its colony. It would lose its sense of purpose. It would become a wandering ant, lost forever. Aren't we all just lost ants wandering through the wilderness trying to find our purpose in life?

As God created and designed insects, He also designed each one of us, and we are all different and unique. We all have many different traits, talents, and ideas. Imagine how great it would be if we all worked together like the ants, sharing and caring for each other.

God intended for us to observe the insects and the other animals to see how they interact with each other. He wanted to set an example for us on how we were supposed to live. He expected us to study and observe our surroundings and take into consideration the intricate detail He laid out before us.

God's design goes far beyond our understanding, yet every single insect and animal plays a vital role in accordance with one another, to help sustain a perfect balance for life on Earth.

The society we live in today is not a part of nature, and we are living in a fast-paced environment not ordinary to the conditions in which we were designed. Since so many of us are unable to connect to nature in the ways we were intended to, we have lost sight of what's most important, which is how to live.

Since we are so disconnected from nature, we have disconnected from our creator. We have isolated ourselves and are now living in a self-evolved bubble. Technology has become the dominating factor in our society, thus creating more distraction from nature and from God.

How can we fix this? How can we go backwards against a society going forward with new technological advancements?

Our cell phones and computers have provided us a way to communicate with one another more than ever before. This is a useful tool to reach out to loved ones if it's used for that purpose. On the other hand, we must ask ourselves what we are mainly using our phones for.

Are we able to disconnect and put our phones away to enjoy a walk through the woods free from distraction? What about enjoying a peaceful evening watching the sun set or gazing up at the stars?

When was the last time we were able to truly appreciate the beauty of nature and listen to the birds sing without the sound of a cell phone buzzing in the background? The question is, are we abusing technology or is it abusing us?

What are we feeding our brain? As we know our thoughts make us who we are and affect our health and relationships, are we monitoring what we watch, read, and listen to on a daily basis?

Our technology exposes us to all sorts of things like pornography, reality TV, different types of music, and social media, which is full of all sorts of negative things. It's a wide open door for negative energy, and it's easily accessible to everyone.

I have always been sensitive to scary movies, and I didn't want to watch them in the past because I was afraid, but now I choose not to because I don't want to invite negative energy into my life.

Why do people watch scary movies? Some say it's because they want to get scared, but why would anyone want to be afraid? Fear is the opposite of love, and when we allow ourselves to feel fear, we are replacing love with that fear. It's very simple: love and fear cannot coexist

God is love and the enemy is fear, so by exposing ourselves to fear, we are inviting the enemy into our lives.

The enemy is very much a part of our world and can disguise himself in many forms. Some forms may be appealing and may seem good, when it is only a deception that takes our attention away from living a godly life.

They say we are saved by grace alone, but what is grace without works? When we decide to live for God, we are inviting Him into our lives to transform our heart mind, and soul, so in order for grace to work through us, we must make sacrifices. The sacrifice to not give into temptation and the sacrifice to be better for God.

Just like our children want us to be proud of them, we too look for approval from our Heavenly Father. When our children do something wrong, they hide it from us, and when we do something wrong, we too hide from God. The difference is that we cannot hide from God, because he sees all and knows every one of our thoughts.

How can we transform our mind so we can live a life of joy, peace, and love? The first step is wanting to, and the second step is to change our lives by feeding our brain positivity, by reading positive stories, watching motivational movies, listening to good music, and being involved in positive activities.

If we are constantly focused on positive things, our thoughts will be positive, which will allow a closer connection to God. In return, the energy we will give off will be positive, and we will attract likeminded individuals into our lives just by making ourselves better.

It's hard living like a true disciple in today's world. We live in a self-serving society and everyone is focused on themselves.

Take social media, for example. It's great to see everyone's pictures, but who is it for? It's for everyone to see, so is it personal? Is that person reaching out to you personally or are you just an observer?

We are all guilty or have been in the past of posting our pictures, opinions, accomplishments, vacations, and daily lives, and then waiting for people to like what we are doing for recognition. When did living our lives need to be recognized by other people and why has it become more important to be recognized by others instead of by God?

What are we doing to others by posting our political views and opinions on who is to blame for the terror in our world? We are creating more enemies and more divide by offending others. What good does it do to blame people for the mess we are in?

We've heard it all before: "those darn liberals," or "those darn Christians." What is this doing? We are stereotyping people based on what they believe in, and putting people into groups. Aren't we all individuals? Don't we all have different minds, hearts, and souls? Why are we all being lumped together?

Don't we all have free will to make our own choices on how to live our lives? With every bad choice we make, there is always a consequence, and instead of using excuses or blaming others, why aren't we holding ourselves accountable?

What are we accomplishing by posting our lives for everyone to see? Are we truly connecting to others, or are we showing off? What would happen if everyone disconnected from social media? We would start to miss certain family members and friends, and we would reach out to each person personally to see how they are doing. We would develop more meaningful relationships. We would plan more family reunions.

Imagine how much better a family reunion would be if everyone was not looking at their phones scrolling through their Instagram or Facebook feed. Imagine how great it would be to sit at a restaurant with our family without cell phones, so we could actually talk and give each other undivided attention.

What example are we setting for the next generation by spending all of our time on the internet? Imagine what people could accomplish if they spent less time on their phones or computers. We would have more time to write letters to loved ones, go hiking, read books, travel, volunteer, and just spend time with friends and family.

There is an invisible wall between us that we think shields us from the outside world, when in fact we are not protecting ourselves—we are closing ourselves off from what we desire most, which is love and acceptance.

We think we are putting ourselves out there by displaying our lives on social media, when in fact, we are only showing the world what we want them to see.

We were designed to have intimate connections with each other, but instead we are only isolating ourselves by interacting through text and social media, causing us to alienate ourselves from others and become lonelier.

Studies have shown that our health relies on human interaction, and the longer we spend living in isolation, the harder it will be to create close meaningful relationships.

As the universe expands faster than the speed of light, all of the galaxies within it are growing further apart, and eventually our galaxy will be isolated and alone, surrounded by darkness.

We too are becoming more distant from each other, through our use of technology and our fast-paced society. Like stars, we are all made of energy and light, and we are all connected, but we seem to think we are separated by our race, religion, and political views.

Emotions are tied into how we feel, and hiding our emotions is what keeps us from connecting to others and knowing who we truly are.

Why are we afraid of showing our emotions? We are all emotional beings, and we all share the same emotions, so why not share them with each other?

When we walk by someone on the street, what's keeping us from saying hello with a warm smile? It's simple: we are afraid of rejection, so instead of opening up to others, we would rather stay closed off from the world.

If we open up to someone and they shun us, the only thing we have to fear is our pride. As we have learned from our Heavenly Father, He teaches us to not have pride or fear, so we should not be afraid to show people who we are by showing our true emotions. We are not fear; we are love.

In order to grow in love, we need to spread our love to others. We are not always going to receive love in return, but an act of kindness is done selflessly. As long as our intentions are selfless we will not be affected by rejection because we were never seeking attention for ourselves in the first place.

Personal connections are important for our health. Who do we connect with on a daily basis and how are we connecting?

How can we silence our thoughts and give someone our undivided attention?

I remember when I was younger, before cell phones were invented, we had a phone on the wall, and if someone called in the middle of dinner, we would let the answering machine get it.

Most of us now have cell phones, and instead of calling, people text each other. Since someone can text us at any time of the day or night, we are constantly being distracted from our present moment. Even if we don't text someone back right away, the thought is in our mind that we need to. We are expected to have our cell phones right next to us at all times for other people's convenience.

How can we unplug from the world and make real connections with our friends and family?

God is with us in each moment, and in order to acknowledge His presence, we need to focus on the stillness of each thought by keeping ourselves grounded and aware of who's right in front of us at the present time.

By allowing ourselves to become present, we are able to see people all around us, and we can make real connections. We can stand in line at the grocery store staring at our phone, or we can talk to a person right behind us, because we never know if that person needed someone to talk to that day and it happened to be one of us.

What does it mean to be a true disciple of Jesus Christ, and what example are we setting for non-believers? Are we serving ourselves or others? What good does it do to go to church if we are not living a Godly life?

Jesus taught His disciples how to live their lives, so how is His teaching any different for us today?

If someone wants to really know God and live the way He intended us to live, the Bible teaches us how to do this: be humble, ask for forgiveness, forgive others, be meek, be gracious, be peaceful, be loving, have self-control, practice goodness, have faith, be gentle, be kind, and be compassionate.

Giving more, living humbly and within limited means, taking care of our planet and God's creation, sharing with each other, leading by example, teaching our children and others through our actions, being thankful for what we have, not wanting for anything, not comparing ourselves to others, not being proud or boastful, and above all, loving God and having his compassion to love everyone— this is how we live the way He intended.

Can we live this way and do we want to? We are given free will, so the choice is up to us, and in order to call ourselves true disciples, we must ask ourselves what it truly means. Are we serving ourselves or are we serving God?

How do we raise the state of our vibration and connect to others if we don't feel like ourselves? Our body needs to be fine-tuned so our true selves can shine through.

I used to wonder how we could live without our bodies, and if we were even the same person when we died. After my experience, I realized our bodies are just vessels we use, and our true selves lie within. In fact, I felt more alive outside my body than when I was in my body, but why is that?

Our bodies are designed to work like machines, and we need to care for our bodies so our spirits can operate at their best. Our spirits get bogged down by our environment which causes us to feel run down. We are affected by what we eat, how much sleep we get, the amount of exercise we do, preservatives, cell phone radiation, and toxins all around us.

After my experience, I read the book, *Health Revelations from Heaven,* by Tommy Rosa and Stephen Sinatra, MD. It's about a plumber who was hit by a car, and while in a coma, he took a journey through Heaven. Throughout his journey, Jesus taught him about how to care for the health of his body in order to allow a closer connection to our Creator and our inner selves.

After reading this book, it only confirmed the validity of my experience by hearing what the plumber had learned. Although he learned all of this while in Heaven, my experience was different, since I was stuck on Earth and aware of my senses.

My out-of-body experience gave me a sense of how scary our environment really is, and we live this way unaware of it because we are accustomed to our surroundings.

I could smell poisons all around me like processed foods, prescription medication, plastic, dish soap, deodorant, shampoo, fabric softener, and many others that I was unaware of before.

Not only could I smell poisons, but I could smell and see dark entities that looked like black shadows. Some of these entities smelled like sulfur or fire, while others smelled like rotting garbage. I noticed these dark entities would cling to people who were unhealthy and would wear them down even more.

What I found most frightening was the vibration and smell coming from my cell phone and my wireless speaker. They emitted an eerie sensation, like nails running across a chalkboard, and they smelled like rotten eggs. Dark entities lingered around them like swarms of flies drawn to honey.

Although my heightened senses only lasted a couple of days, I now make a conscious effort to be more aware of certain products that contain harmful preservatives and buy safer alternatives. I no longer carry my cell phone near my body, and I got rid of my wireless speaker.

We are not going to be able to eliminate every toxin in our environment, but we can keep our bodies healthier. By doing so, we can function at a higher state of vibration in order to not be affected by the poisons in our environment and not attract dark entities.

Most of us know what it takes to be healthy, but our bad habits keep us from creating a healthy lifestyle. If we want to feel our best and develop a closer connection to our Creator and our true selves, then we can with God's help. He will give us the willpower, but then we have to do the rest.

Living in a society so dependent on technology is very difficult, because we are constantly being exposed to it, but if we make a conscious effort to try and limit our use of technology and, instead, be in tune with nature, then we will be better for it and we will set a good example for our future generations.

Searching

Why are we so consumed by what we acquire in life? We spend our whole lives searching for something that's missing. For some people it's acquiring more money, success, fame, and possessions, thinking they will be happier with a bigger house or a better car. Only to realize once they acquire these things, they always take them for granted and are left unsatisfied.

I remember there was a time in my life I wanted to buy a house more than anything. Every time my husband and I would move somewhere to rent a new place, I would always get tired of where we lived. I loved our home in the beginning, but over time I grew tired of it.

I would always want my home to look nice, and I would spend money on furniture and decor items.

I created the perfect image in my mind of how I wanted our life to be and what I thought was most important. I envisioned the perfect house and a nursery all ready for a new baby. I prayed for my daughter for almost seven years, and she ended up coming at a time we least expected it.

She came at a time in our life when we had less money than we had previously. We never bought a house, and there wasn't a perfect nursery set up, and yet we found ourselves happier than we ever imagined. What changed? I realized what was most important was being a family, and it did not matter where we lived, because love has no boundaries.

We are living here on this earth temporarily and our true home is not of this world. The only thing real in this world is "us," the relationships we create, and the love we have for one another. When we focus on each other and not things, our world changes right before our very eyes. Stuff becomes minuscule and we start to see the bigger picture.

People all around us are being stripped of their homes and possessions due to hurricanes, floods, and fires. What happens when you have nothing left but the clothes on your back? Families are reuniting, and strangers are helping others and bringing the community closer together.

Although none of us want to be left homeless, we need to live as though we are already homeless to this world.

When we reevaluate our lives and focus on our family, friends, and neighbors, the background fades away around us like a smoky haze. Instead of focusing on a bigger house or a better car, let's focus on strengthening our relationships and creating new ones. Let's bridge the gaps that divide us by sharing with our community. Let's tear down the walls in our homes, so we can see our neighbors. Let's open our homes by opening our hearts to those around us, because the only thing we can carry home with us when we leave here is each other.

We all know the saying, "beauty is on the inside," and while we acknowledge this truth, do we apply this concept to our lives or are we searching for acceptance?

We live in a very superficial society, and in order for us to feel socially accepted, we feel like we have to look a certain way in order to fit in.

We all know that clothing is for warmth, and it should be used for that purpose, but instead clothing has become a fashion statement and we are all judged based on what we wear.

We are also judged based on our looks, and a lot of people are trying to look younger and are willing to spend thousands of dollars on anti-aging products and plastic surgery. We all are expected to age, so why are we so afraid of the inevitable? When I see an older woman that embraces her age, I think it's a beautiful reminder of her lifelong journey, her accomplishments, and all of the hardships she endured.

Why can't we look at people as they are and not for who we want them to be? We should be able to embrace the natural order of our lives and let ourselves age gracefully the way God intended. When we pass on, our youth will be restored, and we will live an eternity without shame, so we need to focus on our eternal home instead of trying to live in our past.

We are expected to look presentable in today's society, and we must live the way we are accustomed to, but we do not need to overindulge in fashion and buy designer jeans, expensive jewelry, and handbags. We should not be ashamed of showing our true emotions by trapping them under a frozen mask, but instead let our smile lines show the laughter we have shared throughout our years and the tears we have shed.

What are we telling the world by changing our appearance? We are showing the world that we are ashamed of ourselves. We are telling the world we live for others and not for God and that our value lies in this world.

We are all expected to grow old, and instead of being afraid of the future, we should be excited that we are getting closer to reaching our ultimate destination, because our true home awaits us and there is nothing to fear.

In order to see others, we should look past their appearance, and instead look into each other's eyes to see their beautiful souls. Beauty is on the inside after all, and that's what our Heavenly Father wants us to recognize in each other.

What is the difference between love and lust? It's funny when people say they only like a certain "type" of man or woman, and they spend their whole life searching for love in all the wrong places.

Before we meet our mate, we create a perfect image in our mind of who we want our companion to be. What are we doing except being closed minded and not being open to who we meet?

I remember when I met my husband thirteen years ago. It wasn't love at first sight like I saw in the movies, and I was not swept off my feet. He was very shy at first, and I had to get to know him. He was not someone that I would have ever pictured myself with, but I knew he was a good man and my heart was telling me to give him a chance.

Over time our love grew, but like all relationships, we went through many obstacles. I didn't know that it was possible to fall in love with the same person more than once.

A good marriage requires work and that involves trust, communication, faithfulness, compassion, and commitment. A lot of the same characteristics that it takes to have a close relationship with God.

God created man and woman as one. He designed each man and woman differently, so that all of us would have another half to complete us. Although He may give each of us only one soulmate, He gave all of us the opportunity to love one another as He does.

My husband completes me, because he brings out the best in me. I'm never afraid to be myself around him, and I see my true identity through the reflection in his eyes. He is my best friend, and I am not afraid to grow old as long as we can grow old together.

A soulmate is the one person that we choose for life, and it has nothing to do with preferences on looks or a checklist of things we think we want from a person, because they are supposed to complete us, not fulfill our needs.

If people are too busy looking for criteria, or too focused on what they are sexually attracted to, they might miss their chance at love. By establishing a relationship with our Creator, we are able to connect to Him and see others how He sees them, which will enable us to get to know others in a different way.

Love takes effort—it needs time to grow, and it is not driven by lust. When we are focused on physical attributes only, it doesn't last. Eventually we get to know that person and looks start to become meaningless. If we have a relationship with God and we put Him right in the middle of our relationships, He will strengthen our love because we will be united through the Holy Spirit.

It takes true commitment to live a godly life, and it's a lot of work, but we never give up, because our eternal reward is worth more than any earthly desire. It is just as important to strengthen our marriage, by focusing only on the good in each other.

When I find myself feeling down, I always stop and think of the things I'm grateful for. We only feel the need to acquire things when we aren't content, but if we make a list of everything we are thankful for and thank God in the process, we will see our circumstances in a whole new light. Sometimes I just lay in bed after rocking my daughter to sleep and just stare at her and weep, and I thank God for her, my husband, and my son. When I'm being thankful, I always feel God's love surround me. If we stop searching and start living, we can truly be able to appreciate our lives and the people in them.

Moving Forward

We have all heard the phrase "life after death," but what if we thought in terms of "life after life?" If we shifted our mindset like this, we wouldn't stop growing or feel we were heading towards a dead end.

What is age really? Isn't it just a number? When we get to our eternal home, we age according to God's grace and we grow spiritually. What's keeping us from growing here on Earth? I have met some people that are mature beyond their years and some that are older, but who remain stagnant in their spiritual growth.

What's keeping us from growing spiritually? Our past keeps us trapped and unable to move forward. We must let our past go by not reliving our mistakes, and we need to embrace life fully. When we keep learning, our mental state causes spiritual growth.

I remember that before my experience, I was having a hard time growing in my faith because I hit a wall. My religious beliefs were causing me to remain stagnant in my relationship with God. I was stuck in the same routines and constricted by the boundaries that surrounded them.

God expected us to grow by learning from others and sharing our stories, experiences, and knowledge. When we read the same stories from the Bible over and over, we are limiting our minds as if God is not living in our present time.

I am not a prophet, but I did talk to God, and although my story is not in the Bible, I was given a gift, and I experienced what it was like walking in the Garden of Eden for a brief period of time.

After my experience, I read many books about people with similar stories, but my experience allowed me to open up to others instead of being closed minded.

People are so concerned that if we think outside the confounds of what religion has taught us, that God will punish us, and we will not be accepted into heaven, but that couldn't be further from the truth. We have a loving God, and we are expected to grow and open our hearts to others and let others open up to us.

That does not mean that the Bible doesn't hold valuable truth to us because our past is closely linked to our future if we connect the dots. But it is not wrong for us to explore other stories in which people have claimed to have a godly experience.

Reading the Bible is what led me to my experience in the first place because I was willing to read it with an open mind and heart. By opening myself up, I was able to hear God very clearly through his word.

After my experience, I read the book, *Proof of Heaven* by Dr. Eben Alexander. It's about a brain surgeon that contracted E. coli meningitis, a disease that ate away the neocortex of his brain. The part of the brain that controls thought and emotion was not available, yet while in a coma, medically brain dead, he experienced a world beyond ours and met God.

He was a skeptic for most of his life, because his medical knowledge was keeping him closed off from anything beyond what he had learned in his medical training. Even though he heard a lot of miraculous testimonies from many of his patients, he always had a medical explanation for each account and kept himself closed and unable to grow spiritually. In his book he stated, "To truly be skeptical, one must actually examine something and take it seriously."

Ignorance causes us to stay trapped, unable to grow spiritually, and keeps us from connecting to others.

We are here to grow in love, and although this task is easier said than done, we must take steps to get there and connect to those around us.

How can we keep moving forward if we fear our future? We encounter many foretold prophesies that are either in the Bible or other testimonies from prophetic people of our time.

As we know, we can change our destiny based on our choices, but we also need to acknowledge that we have a living God that controls our universe, and He has a plan that works in favor to benefit all of mankind.

In addition to God's plan, He also knows our true intentions. What is the difference between intention and choice?

When Jesus taught his disciples, He knew there was one in his midst that had bad intentions. He did not abandon him or send him away, but shared the same knowledge, truth, and love. He never gave up hope that Judas would turn from his wicked ways, and He waited until the last day before His death and saw the future flash before His eyes of His betrayal. He was able to see the future because the plan had already taken place in the mind of Judas and his intentions were strong.

Jesus knew his destiny was going to lead him to death, but He didn't know when or who would forsake him, until the choice was made. Our minds lead us to our destiny—most of us plan for our future, but it is our intentions that get us there.

God can see not only our intentions, but He is well aware of the enemy's intentions to harm us. Although God works against these schemes, and the plans change, the enemy's intentions do not.

When I think of God at work against the enemy, I visualize a chess game being played, and we are used as the pawns. There are those of us who have good intentions and those who don't, but we are either being used by God or by the enemy, and God needs an army of love. We should not see others as our enemies, but instead, we should acknowledge the enemy that is trying to control those who are lost and learn to love others as God does, through us.

We should not live in fear of the end as it was prophesied by thinking we are running out of time. God taught me that I didn't need to worry or fear the end of time, because his plan will demolish all evil, and by the end of time, good will prevail and we will all be reunited in love.

During my experience, when I had my spiritual awakening, I could feel God's love surging through me, and all I remember thinking was that I wanted others to feel it to. I wanted everyone to know how much God loved them, because I knew it was the kind of love that could heal the world. I realized that we are all capable of it, and if everyone went through what I did, we could all create peace and harmony here on Earth.

I saw a vision of my future, or a future that was possible if I were to choose the path God laid out for me. A community in which my friends and family lived in harmony and shared a way of humble living. Quaint homes, surrounded by nature, growing crops together, plentiful and sustainable for our needs. Sharing with each other and not wanting for anything. A life in which we could live the way God intended. Then one thought hit me like a ton of bricks. Why wait for heaven when we can bring heaven to Earth? God is using each one of us in different ways, and He's paving the way for Jesus through us—our love will light the way. When I envision Jesus' return, I see it as us being a reflection of Him in order to bring an end to all the suffering and pain in the world. Each one of us is a missing puzzle piece, and we all have something valuable to offer.

As we keep moving forward, we must remember the secret to life is love: loving life, nature, people, all living things, and loving God. Connecting love to every aspect of our lives keeps us connected to our life line. Our life line is God and He has everlasting love. If we harness His love and let Him pour His love into our souls, we can spread it to everyone around us.

We can step outside and feel the sun hit our face, close our eyes and imagine soaking up God's love. We can let the light flow through us and energize our souls. Burdens are heavy, and light is not—love and light heal all wounds, and there is a light burning inside each one of us. It just needs to be lit.

We can jump into the cool ocean and let God wash away all of our burdens, refreshing our soul.

We can stand on top of a snow-covered mountain and feel God touch our face through the cool winter breeze, taking away our fear and embracing our love.

We can sit in a grassy orchard under a tall oak tree and listen to God's voice by hearing the branches rustle in the wind and listening to the birds sing.

We can stand in a stable and let our hands run down a horse's mane, feeling God's patience flow through us.

We can run through the rain and breathe in the fresh dewy air, cleansing our soul.

We can walk barefoot along beautiful sandy beaches and let time escape us.

God lives in everything, and we can connect to God anytime through nature by reviving and waking up our soul.

Happiness is reached by appreciation and being content at where we are in the present moment, so let's make our present moment in God's soul because His love is limitless.

Vision of Poems

Stars

Created as stars before we were ever born in his image. Painted with precision, intention, and grace. As each star has an end, it brings forth a new beginning, burning so brightly with love that is bursts. Created from stardust, igniting our hearts and spreading our love, like a sapphire shining in a dark room. As our Creator hovers above us, we enjoy the sun shining upon our face, and remember we are truly loved, and we were intended from the very beginning of time.

Harmony

One instrument playing in harmony with each other. Helping those who are out of tune, by striking a chord in those who are still in silence, as each vibration goes out into the world, each tune has a beam of light and a string of hope, seeking to find the missing pieces of a broken heart. Let our voices soar above the clouds to reach the heavens, connecting to our guiding light. Orchestrating a dance of stars, glowing with love and hope, allowing our minds to shift unto what our hearts desire. As the last trumpet blows and the sun sets in the west, let our gaze be upon the morning song and the silver clouds, as our hearts and souls to bring forth the morning dew. Anxiously waiting, but not eager to leave behind any tunes unturned so we may sing our song in praise in unity forever.

White Dove

One thought and life came forth. A perfect loving soul pure as a white dove. Painting each star in the heavens with precision and grace, and creating every speck of dust with intention and detail. Every creature and every grain of sand designed purposefully. Life flowing together from quiet streams to roaring rivers. Focusing on every detail, while in constant thought, deception flew past like a black crow in a stark sky. A world created, constricted by time, as it must run its course. Brokenhearted and a tear-filled sky waiting for the essence of love to ignite. Lost souls flickering in the moonlight. Blinded by the evil that found its way unto the world. As the tides change course and the current draws near, hope remains. Reminding those without of the beauty that surrounds us. Soaring eagles and autumn leaves blowing in the wind. The sun still shines for all to see, so we can all have grace and let our souls roam free.

Garden of Love

We are all like flowers. Each petal representing the gifts we are given. Each one of us a different color and unique in our own way. Let's be the sunshine in each other's lives and nourish one another with our love, to help each other grow. We all have petals that need to be shed. Let's pull the weeds from our lives by getting rid of our excuses and our pride. By letting go of our burdens, and letting the petals fall where they may. Like the bumble bee that pollinates the flowers, we can affect those around us. We can create change by letting our true colors shine through and forgiving one another. The stronger our faith grows over time, the sooner we can create a colorful garden of love.

Leadership

Great leaders never stop learning. With humble attitudes and gracious hearts, let's learn from those around us. Remembering, we all have special gifts we can share with one another. We are all connected. Let our differences bring us closer together, not further apart. If we are too busy pointing fingers and judging those around us, we won't be able to love them. Focusing on the good qualities in each person, instead of the bad. We can't change someone, but we can inspire those around us that want to change. Let love be our only weapon in life, by being the love and the light. Through small acts of kindness, working together in harmony, to make what's left of this world a better place.

Epilogue

Our journey to Jesus does not happen overnight. It's not the moment we get baptized, the moment we have every Bible verse memorized, or by preaching the word of God.

It's not knowing about God, but truly knowing God, and once we know the Father, we know the Son.

Religion is just a mask we wear to show others how we want to be perceived. The question is not what others see, but what we see when we look at others. Why we feel different emotions toward others and how to change our internal perceptions.

The journey is not to Jesus, but rather through Jesus, because it's the desire to want to be like Him, so He can live through us, and the journey is constant and unwavering.

My journey is in this very moment as I'm typing this page, because it's taking each moment we live our lives trying to be better than we were yesterday.

It's the vulnerability we feel come over us when we are driving to work and we stop to question our existence, what our purpose is in this life, and how we can help others.

Our intentions make us who we are, and why we do the things we do is the question we must ask ourselves.

Are our lives about what will benefit us, or something more? The real journey begins when we take off our masks and start to transform our souls. Working on finding our true selves and finding God who lives within us.

There is a fire burning in all of us, and the discovery is such, as to why some of us feel it, and some don't.

We must embrace our burning desire that yearns for love, and if we learn to love ourselves because we know God does, then we can love others. Each day learning from our mistakes, when we are tested in the midst of anger, through trials and tribulations.

The journey is just that, because it takes time, patience, acceptance of oneself and of others. Growing stronger each day, by the choices we make and the shortcomings that come with it.

Jesus is on the other side of FEAR, and the path that leads to Him is faith that has no boundaries or limitations. God does not expect anything from us, because there are no strings attached to His LOVE.

Our lives here are a journey in which we choose our destiny, but we all reach the same destination, and it's our choice to return to truth, to oneness, and to love.

Made in the USA
San Bernardino, CA
12 April 2019